Table of Contents

Organic soap is simply better for your skin...It contains natural ingredients such as plant-derived base oils, glycerin, and essential oils.By contrast, synthetic, mass-market soap is made of petroleum-based lathering agents, synthetic fragrances, harsh dyes, and dangerous preservatives. It's not surprising, then, that a lot of our customers say that their skin feels better after using organic soap, and that it sometimes helps to improve skin conditions such as eczema and acne, rather than producing further irritation. But not only is organic soap better for you, it's also better for others. It's better for the environment because producing its ingredients has less of an environmental impact, and because those ingredients break down easily and cause fewer problems after they go down the drain.It's better for animals because its ingredients are already recognized as safe, so no animal testing is necessary. And finally, organic soap is better for the economy, because it is often made by small, local producers, so the dollars you spend on it stay in the community. When I talk about organic soap, most of the time I'm talking about natural and organic soap.Natural soap is made out of fats or oils, water, lye, and often essential oils and natural dyes. Organic soap also has the added benefit of being made of ingredients that are produced with organic farming practices, that is, farming practices that don't use pesticides or synthetic fertilizers. So organic soap is natural soap, but it is also one step better.

What is Organic Soap

Organic soap is one of the latest all-natural alternative products that's getting a lot of attention. Organic soap is a soap that is made with only organic materials. A lot of the time organic and natural are used interchangeably and, for many, an all-natural soap is a great alternative. But if you want to truly use an environmentally-friendly soap, then organic is the way to go. Since it's impossible to make soap without lye, and lye is far from organic, there is really no such thing as a truly 100% organic soap. But, with that being said, making sure all your other soap ingredients are organic not only helps the environment, but helps your skin and body as well. Organic soap making is one of those traditional skills that are undergoing a huge renaissance. With many people craving healthier, more natural and more personally crafted skin products, artisan soaps have turned into some very profitable businesses.

How To Make Organic Soap

Part1

Creating the Lye and Oil Solutions

• Use a kitchen scale to properly measure out your ingredients. Having accurately measured ingredients is crucial to making soap successfully. If some of the ingredients are measured incorrectly, the skewed ratio could be significant enough to keep the soap from solidifying or curing properly. If you don't have a kitchen scale, you can purchase one in the kitchen or housewares section at a local department store, or you can order one online through major retailers. Any container, utensils, molds, or pitchers used to measure or make the soap should not be used to work with food.

The contamination caused by the lye would not be safe for consumption.

• Wear protective clothing when working with lye. Lye is caustic and you want to avoid getting it on your skin or near your face. To protect your skin while working with the lye, wear long sleeves, gloves, and goggles. Avoid breathing in the fumes by working near an open window, or by having a fan circulate the air. If you have breathing problems or are concerned about breathing in the lye fumes while working with it, wear a respirator mask. You can purchase one at your local hardware store or online with major retailers.

• Pour 4.5 fl oz (130 mL) of distilled water into a stainless steel pitcher. Use a thick, durable plastic pitcher if you do not have a stainless steel one. Avoid using aluminum, as the lye will negatively react to the element.

• Stir in 2.14 oz (60 g) of food-grade lye to the pitcher with the water. Pour the lye slowly to keep it from plopping into the water. Use a silicone spatula to stir the water as you pour in the lye. Continue stirring the mixture to dissolve the lye. Always add the lye second to the water. Pouring the water directly onto the lye will prematurely start the chemical reaction and heat up the lye.

• Allow the lye solution to cool down for 30-40 minutes. Be careful when handling or transporting the lye solution. The natural chemical reaction of the lye with the water will create a hot solution. When mixed with water, lye can reach temperatures as high as 200 °F (93 °C). Even after you have let it cool down the solution will still be considerably hot—around 100–110 °F (38–43 °C).

• Heat up the coconut oil in a double boiler to melt any solidified parts. Stir the coconut oil over a low heat to keep it from bubbling or burning. Once all solidified remnants of the oil have melted, remove it from the heat. A similar product to coconut oil is babassu oil, which is a vegetable oil that comes from the babassu palm in South America. Use equal amounts of this oil if you are allergic to the coconut oil, or if you want to try something different.

• Mix the oils in a second stainless steel pitcher to make the soap batter. Add 12 fluid ounces (350 mL) of olive oil, 1.5 fluid ounces (44 mL) of castor oil, and 2.5 fluid ounces (74 mL) of melted coconut oil. The castor oil will create the lather in the bar of soap when used, the olive oil will soften and condition your skin, and the coconut oil will help harden the soap. The coconut oil will be hot, so be careful when mixing it with the other oils.

The Most Important Step In Preparing Your Soap-Making Ingredients

• Getting the right scent.

• Measuring your ingredients.

• Using the right type of lye.

• Choosing the right heating element.

Part 2

Mixing the Soap Batter

• Add the lye solution to the pitcher with the oils to make the soap batter. Pour in the mixture slowly to avoid spilling it. Be careful not to burn yourself, as both the lye and the oils are hot. The temperature of the oils and lye solution should be around 100–110 °F (38–43 °C). Use a stainless steel thermometer to check this before mixing the two solutions. If the oil temperature is lower, heat in the double boiler until the temperatures are about the same

• Stir the solution with a stainless steel spoon to combine the ingredients. Any stainless steel spoon will work fine, but it will be easier to stir the mixture if the spoon has a long handle. Continue to gently stir the mixture for about 30 seconds. This will give the lye and oils a chance to mix before you blend them more thoroughly. If you do not have a stainless steel spoon or one with a long enough handle, use an immersion blender in the off-position to gently mix the ingredients.

• Add special clay minerals, sugar, flowers, or herbs to color your soap. Pick an ingredient that will change the appearance of the soap to match your favorite color. As is, the olive oil used to make the soap will give it a yellow or cream color after it is cured. If you enjoy or don't mind that color, don't add extra ingredients. Add in a dash of cosmetic clays to change the soap color to pink, green, or white. Use a couple of drops of milk, cane sugar, or honey to give the soap a warm caramel color. For more vibrant colors, use the petals or leaves from your favorite flowers or herbs. For example, alkanet root will give the soap a purple hue and spinach leaves make the soap green.

• Blend the solution for 1 minute with an immersion or stick blender. Submerge the bladed portion of the immersion blender into the mixture before turning it on; otherwise, the immersion blender will fling the solution out of the pitcher. Slowly rotate the immersion blender around the base of the pitcher to blend the solution. If there are multiple speed settings for your immersion blender, have it on the lowest setting. Quickly pulsating the solution will create unnecessary air bubbles in your soap batter. If you do not have an immersion or stick blender, you can purchase one at a local department store or online.

• Alternate between stirring and blending the batter to thicken it. Use the immersion blender in the off-position to stir the batter. Switching between the spoon and immersion blender may cause you to drip or spill the batter. Continue this process for about 10-15 minutes. For soap making, thickened soap batter is called "trace." This means that the batter is thick enough for you to drip some onto the surface of the batter and have it remain on the surface. When a soap reaches this consistency, it no longer needs to be mixed and is ready to be poured into the mold. Add essential oils to the trace soap batter to give it a desired scent. Start by adding 1 US tbsp (15 mL) of the oil and stir it into the batter using your stainless steel spoon. The essential oils will smell stronger when added to the batter than when the batter is cured. So if the scent is not strong in the batter, add more in small increments until you can smell it. Some common essential oils to add are vanilla, almond, lavender, lemongrass, geranium, or peppermint.

Molding and Curing the Soap

• Pour the batter into a 4 in (10 cm) silicone soap mold to shape it. Use a mold that will create 4 rectangular bars of soap. A standard mold will have an approximate

4 by 4 in (10 by 10 cm) length and width, and 3 in (7.6 cm) height. You can find one of these molds at a local craft store or online with major retailers. Consider getting a silicone mold that has a fun pattern or design on it to further personalize your homemade soap. You can also use a loaf mold that is not sectioned off and just cut the soap into individual bars later. Avoid using muffin tins or baking pans as the soap batter will most likely ruin the tins and the soap.

• Cover the filled mold with freezer paper and a towel to trap the heat. Leave the soap covered for at least 24 hours, but check on it periodically to make sure that it is not overheating and cracking. If it develops cracks, leave it covered, but move it to a cooler location like a dark closet or a cool basement. Use freezer paper over standard wax paper, as freezer paper is thicker and the wax paper might melt against the heat of the soap batter. You can also use parchment paper.

• Uncover the mold and leave it to firm up over the next 2-3 days. Check on the soap at least once a day to make sure that it's hardening properly and has not been disturbed. You will notice that the texture of the soap batter will gradually change to a gelatinous state over the 3 days. By the third day, it should seem fairly firm if you touch it with your finger.

• Pop the soap bars out of the silicone mold to cure them. Place the bars in an area out of direct sunlight, and leave them alone for at least 6-8 weeks. The air will dry out and fully harden the soap. After that time, the soap will be ready for you to use and enjoy. Soaps that use a higher ratio of water to olive oil will only need to be cured for 4-6 weeks instead. If you used a loaf silicone mold, use a knife to carefully cut the loaf of soap into 4 equally sized bars before curing them.

Organic Soap Ingredients

When shopping for skin care products, it is extremely important to thoroughly go through the list of ingredients used. Some companies label their products as natural, but when you review their list of ingredients, it's loaded with chemicals. Most commonly used set of ingredients in organic soaps are:

Base oils

Organic soap is made from natural ingredients, and in most cases, those ingredients are also organically farmed. The majority of the soap bar is made of what are called base oils. We use some of the same base oils for soap making that you can use for cooking. So if it's safe to eat, it's probably also safe to put on your skin. In the case of our latest recipe, those oils are coconut, olive, and castor bean oil. (We used to use palm oil but are phasing it out because of the massive amount of environmental destruction that it takes to produce.)

Essential oil

Another ingredient in our soap is essential oil. Essential oils are the volatile or fragrant compounds in certain plants. Most essential oils are distilled from things you would eat such as citrus fruit or herbs. Two examples of essential oils we use are lemon essential oil and rosemary essential oil. Experts say you shouldn't put pure essential oil on your skin because it is very concentrated and can cause irritation. However, essential oil diluted with another oil is just fine.

Glycerin

Most organic soap also contains glycerin. Glycerin is a natural product of the soap making reaction. A lot of mass-market soap makers and some small-batch soap makers take out the glycerin because it makes the soap bar last longer or because they can sell the glycerin to use in other cosmetic products. However, when glycerin is left in the soap bar, it acts as a humectant, or a substance that attracts moisture from the air into the skin. Two other natural humectants are aloe and honey. And here are some ingredients

• Coconut oil

• Aloe Vera

• Oats

• Peppermint

• Clay

• Turmeric

• Goat's Milk

• Honey

• Olive Oil

• Cinnamon

• Natural Dye

• Lye

Using all natural and organic skin care products is a long term investment in your health because your skin absorbs chemicals and then transfers it to your bloodstream. Skin is the largest organ of the body, deserves the utmost care. It deserves no less than the best quality chemical free products for its nourishment.

Why Organic Soap Contains Lye

In order to take your raw ingredients and turn them into an organic soap, you need to have a chemical reaction. This is where lye comes in. In its natural state it can be dangerous, so it needs to be handled carefully, but once it is mixed in with the other ingredients, and the soap is made, it isn't dangerous at all.

Traditional Soaps Contain Additives

A lot of the additives that are in conventional soap are not only unnecessary, but can be dangerous. Sodium laurel sulfate, a main ingredient in manufactuered soap, was originally intended to clean the grease from car engines. SLS and other surfactants can be extremely drying and irritating, causing skin problems such as itchiness and rashes. Conventional soaps also have a slew of other chemicals in them that can cause irritation and allergic reactions.

Making Organic Soap

Depending on what recipe you use, there are very precise measurements needed for the chemical reaction to take place.

Organic Soap and Allergies

Organic soaps by their very nature are gentler on the skin than soaps made with unnecessary chemicals. With that being said, if you have an allergy to almonds, you will need to stay away from any organic soap made with almonds. But if the soap doesn't have any ingredients in it that are known allergens to you, then you will be fine.

Organic soaps clean just as well as their chemical full counter parts. But what about in comparison to antibacterial soaps. Triclosan, which is the most commonly used ingredient for making a soap antibacterial, is believed to be harmful. But adding certain essential oils to organic soaps can increase their cleaning power and make them antibacterial without having to use harmful chemicals. Tea tree oil is a great antibacterial, as well as lavender and lemon.

Recipe

Ingredients

How To Make Organic Soap With Mustard Seeds

Ingredients

• 6 1/2 oz (184g) Olive Oil

• 3 1/4 oz (92g) Sunflower Oil

• 2 1/2 oz (65g) Palm Oil

• 2 1/2 oz (65g) Coconut Oil

• 1 oz (28g) Sweet Almond Oil

- 1 1/2 oz (40g) Beeswax

- 8 oz (227g) (230ml) Mineral water

- 2 1/4 oz (65g) Lye (Sodium Hydroxide/Caustic Soda)

- 2 teaspoons (7ml) Lemongrass essential oil

- 1 teaspoon (5ml) Lime essential oil

- 1/2 teaspoon (5ml) Rosemary essential oil

- 2 drops Benzoin essential oil

- 2 tablespoons Mustard Seeds

Method

• Prepare a soap mold. If you don't have a specific soap mold, then any good size container will do. Sturdy plastic containers that still have enough give to ease the soap out make the best containers because you don't have to line them. Recently I've been using silicon molds as it's so much easier to remove the soap.

• A quick grease round with a little solid oil from the recipe and they're good to go. Glass, wood, ceramic or cardboard all lined with freezer/butcher paper will also make suitable molds. Avoid using any metal molds unless you can be sure they are stainless steel.

• Put on protective eyewear, mask, apron and long rubber gloves. Pour the mineral water into a large glass/sturdy plastic jug or plastic bucket. Slowly, add the lye (caustic soda), using a plastic spatula to stir until dissolved.

• The water will start to heat when it reacts with the lye, it will need to cool until it reaches the required temperature

• In a large stainless steel or enamel pan, gently melt any oils or waxes over a low heat. (this does not include essential or fragrance oils). Use two candy thermometers place one in the caustic soda mix and one in the oil mix.

• Using a stick blender begin carefully stirring your mixture for several minutes, slowly at first without switching the blender on.

• Reaching The 'Trace' Stage: Then give your mixture a few short 3 second bursts, stirring between each burst until the mixture thickens slightly and looks a little like thick custard.

• Pour your soap into the mold and smooth out using a spatula.

• Place a piece of cardboard over the top of it.

• Wrap an old towel around the whole thing to keep the heat in.

• Allow your soap to set for 24 hours in a warm place until the soap has hardened. Don't be too alarmed if you take a quick peek at your soap and it looks translucent, this is called the gel stage and is perfectly natural. When the soap has hardened (usually around 24 hrs), remove from the mold and allow it to air for a few hours.

• As a general rule, it should be about the consistency of hard cheese before you cut it. The soap will still be caustic at this point so I would recommend still handling it with gloves for the first 48 hours.

• Cut your soap into blocks, for this, you can simply cut by hand for a more rugged look.

• Or use your soap cutting box for something more symmetrical.

• Next cover/line a cooling rack, tray or box with a cloth and stand the soap blocks upright without touching each other so the air can circulate. Store them in a dry ventilated place turning them each day in the first week and then every other day thereafter for 4 weeks.

• This time continues the curing process ensuring that all of the lye has been neutralized and water evaporated. During this time you may find a fine dust on your soap, this is soda ash and can be scraped off before use.

• All of the cold process soap recipes on Savvyhomemade allow 5% superfatting. This ensures correct saponification (the reaction that creates soap) making sure there is zero free caustic alkali remaining and a good ph balance is achieved.

Organic Soap With Seaweed

Ingredients

- 8 1/2 oz (240g) Olive Oil

- 1 1/2 oz (40g) Avocado Oil

- 2 oz (50g) Coconut Oil

- 2 oz (50g) Palm Oil

- 1 oz (30g) Beeswax

- 6 oz (170g) Mineral water

- 2 oz (55g) Lye (Sodium Hydroxide/Caustic Soda)

- 1 1/2 teaspoons (7ml) Grapefruit essential oil

- 1 teaspoon (6ml) Orange essential oil

- 1 1/2 teaspoon (2ml) Petitgrain essential oil

- 2 tablespoons (1/2 oz)(15g) of Dried Seaweed

Method

- Prepare a soap mold. If you don't have a specific soap mold, then any good size container will do. Sturdy plastic containers that still have enough give to ease the soap out make the best containers because you don't have to line them. Recently I've been using silicon molds as it's so much easier to remove the soap.

• A quick grease round with a little solid oil from the recipe and they're good to go. Glass, wood, ceramic or cardboard all lined with freezer/butcher paper will also make suitable molds. Avoid using any metal molds unless you can be sure they are stainless steel.

• Put on protective eyewear, mask, apron and long rubber gloves. Pour the mineral water into a large glass/sturdy plastic jug or plastic bucket. Slowly, add the lye (caustic soda), using a plastic spatula to stir until dissolved.

• The water will start to heat when it reacts with the lye, it will need to cool until it reaches the required temperature

• In a large stainless steel or enamel pan, gently melt any oils or waxes over a low heat. (this does not include essential or fragrance oils). Use two candy thermometers place one in the caustic soda mix and one in the oil mix.

• Using a stick blender begin carefully stirring your mixture for several minutes, slowly at first without switching the blender on.

• Reaching The 'Trace' Stage: Then give your mixture a few short 3 second bursts, stirring between each burst until the mixture thickens slightly and looks a little like thick custard.

• Pour your soap into the mold and smooth out using a spatula.

• Place a piece of cardboard over the top of it.

• Wrap an old towel around the whole thing to keep the heat in.

• Allow your soap to set for 24 hours in a warm place until the soap has hardened. Don't be too alarmed if you take a quick peek at your soap and it looks translucent, this is called the gel stage and is perfectly natural. When the soap has hardened (usually around 24 hrs), remove from the mold and allow it to air for a few hours.

• As a general rule, it should be about the consistency of hard cheese before you cut it. The soap will still be caustic at this point so I would recommend still handling it with gloves for the first 48 hours.

• Cut your soap into blocks, for this, you can simply cut by hand for a more rugged look.

• Or use your soap cutting box for something more symmetrical.

• Next cover/line a cooling rack, tray or box with a cloth and stand the soap blocks upright without touching each other so the air can circulate. Store them in a dry ventilated place turning them each day in the first week and then every other day thereafter for 4 weeks.

• This time continues the curing process ensuring that all of the lye has been neutralized and water evaporated. During this time you may find a fine dust on your soap, this is soda ash and can be scraped off before use.

• All of the cold process soap recipes on Savvyhomemade allow 5% superfatting. This ensures correct saponification (the reaction that creates soap) making sure there is zero free caustic alkali remaining and a good ph balance is achieved.

Ingredients

• Coconut oil ⅔ cup – to produce good lather

• Olive oil ⅔ cup – which makes a hard and mild bar

• Other liquid oil ⅔ cup – like almond oil, grapeseed, sunflower or safflower oil

• ¼ cup lye – also called 100% sodium hydroxide

• ¾ cup cool water – use distilled or purified

Instructions

• Cover your work area with newspaper. Put your gloves and other protective wear on. Measure your water into the quart canning jar. Have a spoon ready. Measure your lye, making sure you have exactly ¼ cup. Slowly pour the lye into the water, stirring as you go. Stand back while you stir to avoid the fumes. When the water starts to clear, you can allow it to sit while you move to the next step.

• In the pint jar, add your three oils together. They should just make a pint. Heat in a microwave for about a minute, or place the jar of oils in a pan of water to heat. Check the temperature of your oils it should be about 120° or so. Your lye should have come down by then to about 120°. Wait for both to cool somewhere between 95° and 105°. This is critical for soap making. Too low and it'll come together quickly, but be coarse and crumbly.

• When both the lye and oils are at the right temperature, pour the oils into a mixing bowl. Slowly add the lye, stirring until it's all mixed. Stir by hand for a full 5 minutes. It's very important to get as much of the lye in contact with as much of the soap as possible. After about 5 minutes, you can keep stirring or you can use an immersion blender (like this). The soap mixture will lighten in color and become thick. When it looks like vanilla pudding it's at "trace" and you're good to go. (Watch this video to see what trace looks like.)

• Add your herbs, essential oils or other additions at this point. Stir thoroughly to combine. Pour the mixture into mold(s) and cover with plastic wrap. Set in an old towel and wrap it up. This will keep the residual heat in and start the saponification process. Saponification is the process of the base ingredients becoming soap.

• After 24 hours, check your soap. If it's still warm or soft, allow it to sit another 12-24 hours. When it's cold and firm, turn it out onto a piece of parchment paper or baking rack. If using a loaf pan as your mold, cut into bars at this point. Allow soap to cure for 4 weeks or so. Be sure to turn it over once a week to expose all the sides to air (which is not necessary if using a baking rack). For a DIY soap drying rack, I took an old potato chip rack and slid cardboard fabric bolts (from a fabric store) through the rungs.

• When your soap is fully cured, wrap it in wax paper or keep it in an airtight container. Hand made soap creates its own glycerin, which is a humectant, pulling moisture from the air. It should be wrapped to keep it from attracting dust and debris with the moisture.

Tips

• To get a good idea of the size of mold needed add together the oils and water in the recipe and then fill a mold with that amount of water.

• The best way to line your mold when using the freezer/butcher paper is to cut two strips, one to go across the width of your box and the other going across the length. Leave enough on the paper to fold over the edges and secure with tape.

• I make a lot of soap and I found a great little tip that helped out. This was to buy a simple, cheap plastic cutlery bin from Amazon. As you can see in the photo it's a great half-moon shape and was perfect for the goats milk soap. It also has a little give in it to help ease the soap out. It makes around 10 large bars per compartment... Perfect for making multiple batches of soap

Possible Problems

If your soap does not harden or just hasn't turned out quite as well as you expected it to, or maybe you forgot to add something. Then you may be able to rebatch it by melting it down and adding any missing, or miss calculated ingredients. If your batch is too lye heavy, making it very brittle and crumbly or if your lye and oils have separated (you will notice a layer of liquid on the top or underneath the soap) I would encourage you to discard it.

How to Make Natural Organic Soap For Face and Body

Soap Making

The Basics

Soap making can be very simple or you can make it as complicated as you like. First, the beauty of making your own is that you can make it with the ingredients that you choose and the fragrances that you like. And adjustments aren't hard but do take some practice. Further, most homemade soap recipes use ounces or grams and ingredients must be weighed to get good results. But I've found a way to simplify the process by converting the ingredients to cups and portions of cups. Consequently, it's much easier and you get the same results time after time.

Lye in Homemade Soap

The one thing in homemade soap you can't substitute is lye. You should always use 100% sodium hydroxide, or lye in crystal form. Don't substitute liquid lye or drain cleaners such as Drano. These may cause inaccurate measurements or have bits of metal in them. You don't want either. Lye is caustic. It can eat holes in fabric and cause burns on your skin. Always be extra careful when using lye. Use gloves and eye protection and a mask if desired. When you mix the lye with water, it will heat up and fume for about 30 seconds to a minute. It may cause a choking sensation in your throat. Don't worry, it's not permanent and will go away after a few minutes. Always add lye to water (not water to lye), and start stirring right away. If allowed to clump on the bottom, it could heat up all at once and cause an explosion.

No Lye in Finished Soap

Even though lye is caustic and dangerous to work with, after it reacts with the oils in your soap (through a process called saponification), no lye will remain in the finished product. The lye reacts with the oils, turning what starts out as a liquid into blocks of soap. When made properly, no lye remains in the finished product.

Homemade Organic Soap Making Equipment

• When learning how to make soap, remember to use equipment that will not be used for cooking. While you could clean everything really well, it's best not to take a chance.

• Stainless steel, tempered glass, and enamel are all good choices for mixing bowls. Don't use copper or aluminum, they will react with the lye. Some plastics may melt, so don't use plastic bowls.

• For spoons, use styrene plastic or silicone. For molds, you can get soap molds at your local craft store or online here, or use silicone baking pans (like this). These are great because you can peel the mold right off. Other things you want to have are a pint and a quart canning jar, newspaper, a stainless steel thermometer that reads between 90° and 200° (find it here), an old towel, and any additions you want to add to the soap.

New parents only want the best for their baby. Manufacturers of baby products, especially baby wash and shampoo, cater to this desire with wholesome pictures of giggly, photogenic babies frolicking in tubs of bubbles. The real picture is not so idealistic. A 2009 study commissioned by the Environmental Working Group showed cancer-causing chemicals in the majority of children's bath products. Formaldehyde and 1,4-dioxane were among the most common contaminants. Fortunately, it's relatively easy to make your organic baby soap bars free of harsh chemicals. Use these bars for your own children, or give them out as baby shower favors.

• Purchase your ingredients from reputable suppliers and choose organic essential oils that are safe for babies and toddlers. Use true essential oil, not perfume oil or massage oil. Valerie Ann Worwood, author of "The Complete Guide to Essential Oils and Aromatherapy," suggests lavender, chamomile, yarrow or dill.

• Fill the double boiler with water and set it on your stove to boil. If you don't own a double boiler, you can improvise by filling a large pot with water and nesting a slightly smaller metal bowl or pot above it.

• Chop up your organic soap base into smaller pieces while the water is coming to a boil. Chopping up the large block of soap base ensures it will melt more evenly. Place the soap chunks into the top of the double boiler (or into the bowl if you're improvising) and cover with a lid.

• Monitor the soap chunks carefully as they melt -- it could take up to an hour. Lift the lid occasionally and stir the chunks with a spoon or spatula. Add your essential oil when the soap base has completely melted. Use 1/4-oz. of essential oil per pound of base. When in doubt, use the essential oil more sparingly, especially for newborns.

• Prepare your soap mold. Line a cardboard box, such as a shoebox or pizza box, with freezer paper. The shiny side of the freezer paper should be facing the soap for easier removal. Overlap the freezer paper if necessary so that there are no gaps. Alternatively, you may use plastic cling wrap to line the box. If you don't want to make your own mold you can buy ready-to-use soap molds from a supplier or craft store.

• Pour the melted soap base into your mold and allow it to cool and harden. This generally takes at least 24 hours.

• Remove the block of finished soap from the mold. Use a ruler or a straightedge to mark where you plan to cut the soap into bars. Cut the soap into smaller bars using firm but gentle pressure. Wrap the bars in paper. You may wish the decorate the bars with ribbon or other embellishments if you're giving them out as favors or gifts.

Things You Will Need

• Organic soap base

• Essential oils, such as lavender or chamomile

• Double boiler or two pots

• Spoon or spatula

• Small cardboard box or commercial soap mold

• Freezer paper or plastic cling wrap

• Straightedge

• Knife

• Paper and ribbon (optional)

Tip

Spray a cotton ball with cooking spray and go over the inside of your mold with it. This will help the finished soap release from the mold more easily.

Warning

Be careful when pouring the soap base into your mold as it will be very hot. It's even OK to let it cool a bit before pouring into the mold you just don't want it to solidify in the double boiler.

Why You Avoid Store-Bought Soap

Most commercial bar soaps at the store are closer to detergent than actual soap because they've stripped out the glycerin in order to sell it (more profit) but this soap doesn't contain the moisturizing benefits found in glycerin. They also contain synthetic dyes, fragrances, and other additives many of us want to stay away from.

Store-bought soap is harsher on the skin and I find it feels like it leaves a layer behind. When I use homemade soap I notice a difference immediately.

How to Make Soap: The Additives

There are as many variations of soap as there are colors in the rainbow. You can literally do almost anything. Here are the basics of additives:

Herbs

All herbal material must be dried. Lavender is popular, as well as chamomile. I love lemongrass and oakmoss, though not together. Use about ¼ cup of dried plant material per batch of this size. (Find high quality dried herbs here.)

Essential Oils

Essential oils are from plants. They come from the roots, stems, flowers or seeds. Fragrance oils can be blends of essential oils or they can be artificially produced. Be sure you know what you have. Most oils can be used at the rate of 15-20 drops or around a teaspoon per batch of this size. (Find 100% pure essential oils here.)

Colors

Natural colors are easy. Use cinnamon or cocoa powder for a brown soap, powdered chlorophyll for green, turmeric for yellow and beetroot for orange. However, sometimes things change colors, like magenta beet powder turning yellowish orange. I would avoid food colors since they don't hold up well in soap. Check out our article, 44 Ways to Color Homemade Soap Naturally, for even more ideas.

Other Items

This would include aloe vera gel, oatmeal, dry milk powder, clays, cornmeal, ground coffee, salt and anything else you may want to use.

Benefits

In this book, I'm going to talk about why organic soap is the best choice if you're concerned not only about what sort of products you put on your skin, but also, the greater impacts of the production and disposal of those products. Organic soap is generally better for the environment, for animals, and for the local economy. Technically, mainstream or non-organic soaps like beauty soap, whitening soap, anti-aging soaps, and other similar soap are no less than harsh detergents packed with harmful ingredients; sometimes even steroids which can lead to skin allergies, reaction to chemicals, skin sensitivity. Organic soap can help you minimize or even avoid this casual toxin exposure and absorption.

Organic is Better for Environment

Organic means there will be no toxin waste to dispose of into the environment. No potentially lethal pesticides or chemical fertilizers are used to grow organic products. This reduces air, soil, and water pollution; hence, organic soaps are ecosystem friendly.

Cruelty-Free

Organic soaps are mostly cruelty-free. They do not use animal fat and are not tested on animals.

More Economic

Besides personal and environmental safety, organic soaps also have a good impact on the economy. It has various social benefits. Since most of the organic products are made by crafters individually in the local community or local market, so the majority of the money circulates within the same community. A consumer can easily access the producer directly at a local craft or a farm market.

Organic is Healthier

Organic products are not only healthy to consume but also to produce. The process of producing organic products does not involve the use of any chemical sprays, fertilizers, or animal experimentation. Hence it's a cycle of healthy production, consumption, and disposal because what goes around comes around.

 It has Better Healing Properties

Due to its natural ingredients like essential oils, aloe, coconut oil, turmeric, honey, etc; organic soaps tend to have additional healing properties for skin conditions such as acne, eczema, and sunburn.

Easily Disposed

As there are no chemical preservatives and toxins involved in the production, once the product is used, the leftover is easily disposed of. Organic raw material or used products are easy to dispose of as compared to chemical products.

Organic soap has Glycerine

In non-organic commercially sold soap glycerine is extracted and used in other products such as body lotions and creams. However, in organic soaps, glycerine is used as a major ingredient. When it comes to your skin, glycerine is the best moisturizing agent. Not only does it retains the moisture but also provides a soft touch to your skin. Use of glycerine is one of the factors that contribute to the high cost of organic soaps.

It is loaded with Antioxidants

Organic soaps preserve the antioxidant properties of the ingredients being used. This can make a big difference because antioxidants help in slowing the skin's aging process and helps in rejuvenating the skin. Antioxidants leave your skin looking younger and fresh.

No Chemical Antibacterial Toxins

Non-organic antibacterial soaps contain chemicals like triclosan, paraben, and other toxic petrochemicals that disrupt the hormones in humans and is harmful to the reproductive system as well. Organic soaps use natural antibacterial like tea tree and peppermint essential oils. These do not have any adverse effect. These essential oils also add up to the aroma and provide aromatherapy in addition to cleansing the skin.

Easy to customize

Organic soaps are not mass produced and do not use preservatives, which limits its shelf life. Since organic soaps are produced in small batches at a local level, it can be easily customized to fit the customers' requirements. The consumers have a variety of aroma, texture, color, shape, and size to choose from. It can be grainy with a dash of peppermint or smooth with coffee and cinnamon aroma.

Maintain PH level

The PH level of organic soaps is almost 9 to10, which means that organic soaps are not so harsh and are gentler on the skin. Use of natural ingredients such as coconut oil not only provides moisture to the skin but also maintains the ph level of your skin.

No Preservatives

The limited shelf life of organic products is because it's all natural without any additional preservatives. This is a good thing because mostly preservatives are chemicals that harm our health.

An ideal choice for Vegans

Since organic soaps rely more on using botanical extracts and herbs to achieve the target, it is an ideal choice for vegans. Mostly organic soaps do not use animal fats. Instead, coconut and palm oil are used as base oil along with essential oils extracted from a variety of flowers (rose, lavender), plants(tea tree, peppermint), spices(cinnamon, clove) and even fruits such as lemon and orange.

Better Production

One reason organic soap is better for the environment is that its plant-based ingredients are grown without pesticides or chemical fertilizers. There is a ton of writing on why these substances are harmful so I'm just going to give a couple examples. Pesticides and artificial fertilizers can kill beneficial insects along with the ones that damage crops, they can harm other animals and plants, they can contaminate soil and water, and they can make people sick if they are exposed directly.

Better Disposal

Another reason organic soap is better for the environment is that it breaks down easily after it is washed down the drain. Some of the ingredients that are bad for you in mass-market soap are also bad for fish and other organisms. Compounds such as parabens that mimic hormones are especially harmful, as they can disrupt these creatures' life cycle.

Better For Animals

Organic soap is better if you're concerned about animals for a couple different reasons. For one, most organic soap is not made out of animals! There are some natural soaps that do use animal fat such as lard or tallow. If you're looking to avoid these ingredients, check the labels, and look up the ingredients if you're not sure. Sometimes ingredients are listed under names such as sodium lardate or sodium tallowate, which are the technical names for the free fatty acid salts that make up soap. Organic soap is also better for animals because usually, no animal testing is required. Organic soap ingredients are listed by the FDA as GRAS, or generally recognized as safe, and most new recipes are simply variations on older ones.

Better for the Economy

Finally, organic soap has greater social benefits beyond personal safety and the environment. Most organic soap is made in small batches by local crafters. Studies have shown that the majority of money spent in local businesses stays within the community. At farmer or crafter markets, you can buy directly from the producer and attach a face to the product. And even if they don't sell directly at markets, usually small-batch makers are more accessible than their corporate counterparts in case you have questions or suggestions for improvement.

Now that we've talked about some of the good stuff in organic soap, I'm going to mention a few of the bad things found in mass-market commercial soap. Three ingredients I'm going to examine are surfactants, parabens, and artificial frangrances.

Surfactants

Surfactants are the chemicals responsible for the cleansing properties of a particular product. Surfactants are made of long molecules with two different ends. One end of the molecule sticks to water, while the other sticks to dirt and oil. Surfactants, as a category aren't automatically bad for you. Soap is technically a surfactant. But you have to be careful about which surfactants you put on your body. One of the most common surfactants in personal cleansers and shampoos is sodium lauryl sulfate. Sodium lauryl sulfate, or SLS, is made from coconuts, but it is contaminated with toxic byproducts when it is manufactured. SLS has been linked to skin irritation, toxicity, endocrine disruption, and cancer. Another unsettling fact about SLS and many other synthetic substances is that your body doesn't have the enzymes to break them down, so they may accumulate in your tissues over time.

Parabens

Parabens are a specific type of preservative used in a wide range of cosmetics and pharmaceutical products. More specifically they prevent growth of mold and bacteria. Paraben is actually short for "parahydroxybenzoate." The reason we should avoid parabens is because they act like estrogen in the body. Too much estrogen can lead to breast cancer and reproductive issues. One piece of good news is that there are a lot of newer safer preservatives available, so a company that is still using parabens is really just being lazy. When inspecting labels on cosmetic products you should look out for the three most common parabens: butylparaben, methylparaben and propylparaben. Or you can just opt for a simple, natural product such as organic soap!

Artificial Fragrances

Let me tell you a story about artificial fragrances. Back in the early days of Metaphor Organic, we used some of them. (Hangs head in shame.) We bought all our essential oils down the street at a little bulk herb shop, and the artificial fragrance oil was right next to the essential oils. We didn't know any better! But the more research we did, the more we realized we should phase them out. For example, there was an artificial vanilla that we used in some of our scent blends. Then we tried to find natural vanilla, but it was very expensive and it didn't smell very distinctly. So we wrote to the manufacturer of the artificial vanilla to try to find out what was in it, because maybe then we could justify putting it in the soap. But they wouldn't tell us! Artificial fragrances recipes are protected as trade secrets. So maybe they are fine, but other sources report that the majority of artificial fragrances are derived from petroleum.

Herbal Organic Soap Making Instructions

Soap seems like it shouldn't be a complicated product, but commercially-produced soap often contains a long list of unnecessary synthetic ingredients. Some of these commonly used ingredients, such as triclosan, are actually toxic. In addition, synthetic fragrances may also cause dermatitis, hormone disruption or respiratory problems; organic herbal soap is a much healthier choice. Making your own soap is not that difficult if you start with with an organic soap base. You may even wish to make an extra large batch and give some homemade organic soaps as gifts.

Overview

The benefits of making your own organic herbal soap are many. You can control exactly what ingredients go into your soap; start by searching out reputable suppliers that sell high-quality ingredients. Although there are many different recipes for organic herbal soap, the easiest ones involve using soap base and dried herbs or essential oils. If you choose to add herbal notes in the form of essential oils, make sure you purchase 100 percent essential oil and not perfume oil.

Tools

Soap making involves a few basic tools you probably already have around your kitchen. In "The Herb Companion," writer Sandy Maine suggests rounding up a double boiler, measuring cups and spoons, some stirring spoons and sticks, and containers to act as molds. Frugal-minded soap makers may choose to line a cardboard box, such as a pizza box, with freezer paper or plastic wrap to create a mold. Line the box with the freezer paper facing shiny side up if you choose this method.

Soap Base

Soap base is available in large blocks that need to be melted down. Soap bases vary in their composition; some are made from coconut and palm oils, others from glycerin. Consult your recipe and purchase organic soap base to ensure the purest product. Chop up the block of soap base so that it will melt more consistently. Boil water in the bottom pot of the double boiler and add the chunks of soap base to the top pot; stir the chunks to help them melt. After the chunks have melted, add the dried herbs or essential oils.

Herbal Ingredients

When adding the botanical elements, more is not necessarily better, especially if the final product will be used by babies or toddlers with sensitive skin. Generally, about 1/4 ounce of oil should be added for each pound of base. Natural, dried herbs are a great addition as well. Chamomile and lavender are prized for soaps and body products. In fact, The University of Maryland Medical Center reports that lavender and chamomile may help relieve insomnia and anxiety. Even if you just like an herb's particular scent, you can easily customize your bars by adding your favorite herbs to the melted soap base. Try adding two or more types of herbs to create your own unique combinations.

Finishing Steps

Pour the melted soap base into the mold once you've added your herbs. Allow the soap to dry at least 24 hours before removing it from the mold. Cut the soap into smaller pieces, and wrap each piece carefully for future use.

Conclusion

After going through all these reasons, it's easy to see why organic soap is a great choice. When we started, it was also the beginning of a larger maker movement, as producers and consumers shift back to smaller, more local, more unique products. Organic soap is perhaps the quintessential small batch local product.